ULTIMATE STICKER COLLECTION

How to use this book

Read the captions then find the sticker that best fits the space. (Hint: check the sticker labels for clues!)

•

There are lots of fantastic extra stickers for creating your own scenes throughout the book.

Penguin Random House

Written by Julia March
Edited by Tori Kosara and Rosie Peet
Designed by Anna Formanek, Sam Bartlett, James McKeag and Anna Pond

Dorling Kindersley would like to thank Randi Sørensen, Heidi K. Jensen, Paul Hansford, and Martin Leighton Lindhardt at the LEGO Group.

First published in Great Britain in 2019 by
Dorling Kindersley Limited
80 Strand, London WC2R 0RL.
A Penguin Random House Company

10 9 8 7 6 5 4 3 2 1
001–312559–Jan/2019

Page design copyright © 2019 Dorling Kindersley Limited
DK, a Division of Penguin Random House LLC

DORL41295

Manufactured by Dorling Kindersley 80 Strand, London, WC2R 0RL under licence from the LEGO Group.

A CIP catalogue record for this book is available from the British Library.

ISBN: 978-0-2413-6046-0

Printed and bound in China

A WORLD OF IDEAS:
SEE ALL THERE IS TO KNOW

www.dk.com
www.LEGO.com

APOCALYPSEBURG

Bricksburg is in ruins! DUPLO® aliens have attacked, leaving the city a brick-strewn wasteland. This gloomy place now has a new name – Apocalypseburg.

Dusty ruins
The attacks have left many buildings smashed and broken. All over the city, dust and dirt float in the air.

Emmet
Emmet Brickowski is a construction worker in Apocalypseburg. His bright smile matches his vibrant orange construction outfit.

Rebuilding
Citizens do their best to rebuild the city after each attack. Repairing the giant Statue of Liberty could take some time!

Thricycle

Emmet drives an awesome triple-decker bike called a thricycle. It gives him a great view over Apocalpyseburg.

The thricycle is built from bricks, wheels and other items Emmet salvaged from the city's ruins.

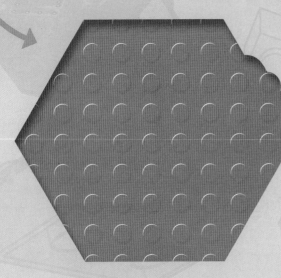

Lucy and Emmet

Special best friends Emmet and Lucy stand by each other through thick and thin. They are ready to defend the city together.

3

EMMET AND FRIENDS

Life in Apocalypseburg can be tough, but Emmet always stays cheerful. He does his best to smile through the hard times and help his friends stay upbeat.

Sweet-toothed Emmet

Emmet takes his coffee with just a touch of cream – and 25 sugars!

Lucy

Lucy is Emmet's best friend. Unlike Emmet, she is tough, cautious and wary of strangers.

Benny

Benny is a friendly spaceman with a cracked helmet. Lack of oxygen sometimes makes him lightheaded.

Unikitty

Unikitty is part kitten, part unicorn. She knows what would brighten up dreary Apocalypseburg – glitter!

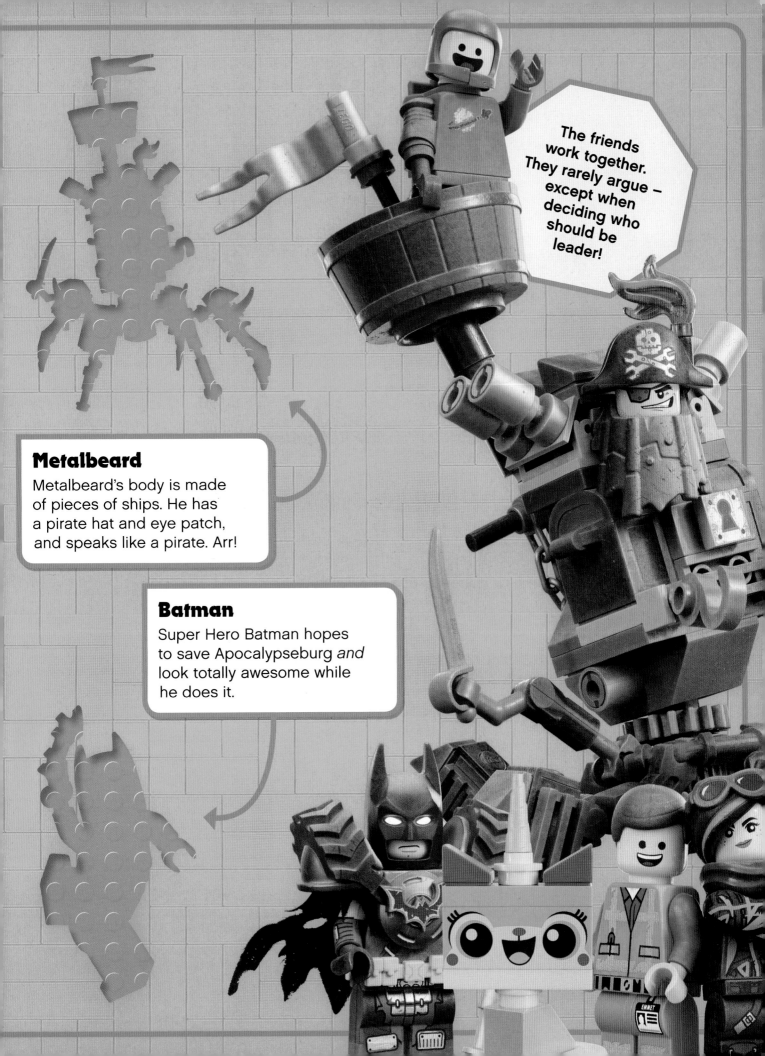

The friends work together. They rarely argue – except when deciding who should be leader!

Metalbeard

Metalbeard's body is made of pieces of ships. He has a pirate hat and eye patch, and speaks like a pirate. Arr!

Batman

Super Hero Batman hopes to save Apocalypseburg *and* look totally awesome while he does it.

ALIENS ATTACK

The DUPLO® aliens attack from the sky. They smash buildings, gobble up bricks and then fly off.
Can anyone stop them?

Gift of bricks

Emmet offers the DUPLO aliens some bricks. He thinks that if he is nice to them, they might stop attacking.

Run, Emmet, run!

The DUPLO aliens do not want to be friends. They take Emmet's bricks and chase him through the city. Look out!

Monster march

The alien monsters march all over the city, knocking down buildings and guzzling all the bricks they can eat.

Citizens flee

The aliens crush everything in their path. Citizens and their pets must run and hide until they have gone.

Strange beings

Aliens from the planet DUPLO come in many shapes and sizes. All of them have big, round eyes.

After filling up with bricks, the monsters fly away. But sooner or later, they return, as hungry as ever.

LUCY

Lucy is strong, courageous and protective. She wants to keep her friends and Apocalypseburg safe from the DUPLO® aliens.

Bold Lucy
Lucy thinks she must act tough to survive in Apocalypseburg. It is such a rough city!

Protective friend
Protecting Emmet from harm is Lucy's main goal. She always encourages her friend to toughen up a little.

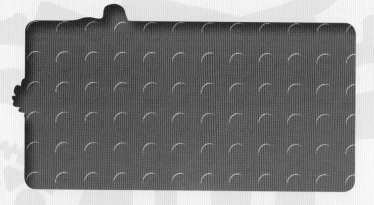

Gloomy thoughts
Lucy often worries about the future. Emmet does his best to cheer up his special best friend.

Happy family
Emmet built a house for himself, Lucy, Unikitty and Planty. But DUPLO aliens flattened it before they could move in!

Whoa there!
A big, angry cat like Ultrakatty can be hard to control. Luckily, Lucy is an expert at kitty-back riding.

Lucy dresses in dark colours – they often suit her mood! But she always wears her bright red goggles.

GETAWAY CAR

When the DUPLO® aliens attack, Emmet and Lucy have to think fast. They use brick rubble and wheels to build a speedy getaway car.

Emmet and Lucy are both Master Builders. They use the bricks around them to build whatever they need.

Super turbo engine

A turbo engine roars at the rear of the car. It might just be powerful enough to outpace an alien ship.

Big wheels

Three of the wheels are from Emmet's thricycle. The aliens blew up the triple-decker bike while Emmet was riding it!

Emmet at the wheel

Emmet drives, while Lucy takes the passenger seat. She tells him which way to steer to avoid the destructive aliens.

Extra features

The car has lots of cool details. It has heat-seeking missiles, a blaster cannon and a scary skull warning sign.

MEET UNIKITTY

Unikitty is a pink kitten with a unicorn's horn. She's as sweet as pie until someone upsets her. Then, Unikitty becomes big, bad Ultrakatty!

Kitty and friends

Unikitty is friends with Emmet and Lucy. All three want to stop the DUPLO® aliens from attacking their city.

Fierce feline

To protect the city, Unikitty transforms into a huge, roaring fighting machine known as Ultrakatty.

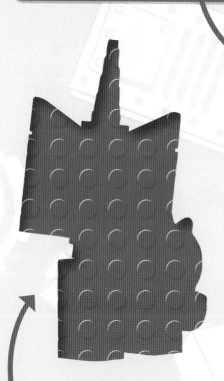

Getting angry

Unikitty is usually very happy. If something makes her mad, she becomes Angry Kitty.

Big battle cat

Giant-size Ultrakatty is a fierce fighter. Lucy rides her when they battle the aliens alongside their friends.

Ultrakatty has very sharp claws. Clinging to Lucy and Emmet's car is easy for her.

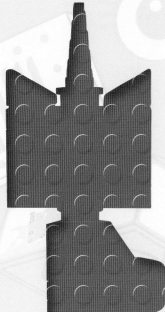

Cute kitty

As soon as the battle is over, Ultrakatty returns to her usual cute, pink, purring form – Unikitty.

SWEET MAYHEM

General Sweet Mayhem commands the DUPLO® aliens. The mysterious space pilot is from the Systar System – and she is not very sweet!

Talking stars

Stars are part of Sweet Mayhem's armoury. They sweet-talk kind people, like Emmet, into doing what they ask.

Sticky situation

Even Batman cannot dodge Sweet Mayhem's stickers. He gets well and truly stuck!

Sticker gun

The general captures foes by blasting cute stickers at them until they cannot move.

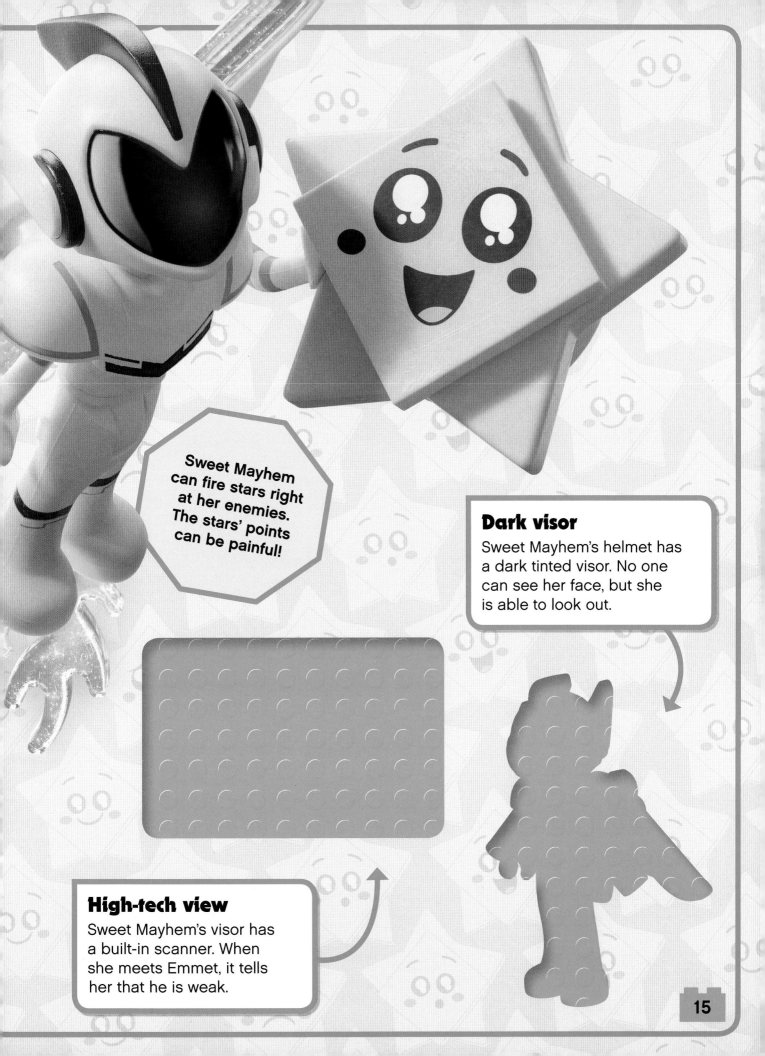

Sweet Mayhem can fire stars right at her enemies. The stars' points can be painful!

Dark visor

Sweet Mayhem's helmet has a dark tinted visor. No one can see her face, but she is able to look out.

High-tech view

Sweet Mayhem's visor has a built-in scanner. When she meets Emmet, it tells her that he is weak.

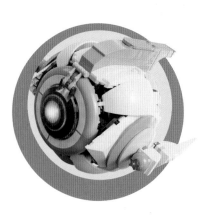

THE *FORMIDABALL*

Sweet Mayhem's spaceship is named the *Formidaball*. It is easy to see why! It has a fierce, formidable array of technology, and it is shaped like a ball.

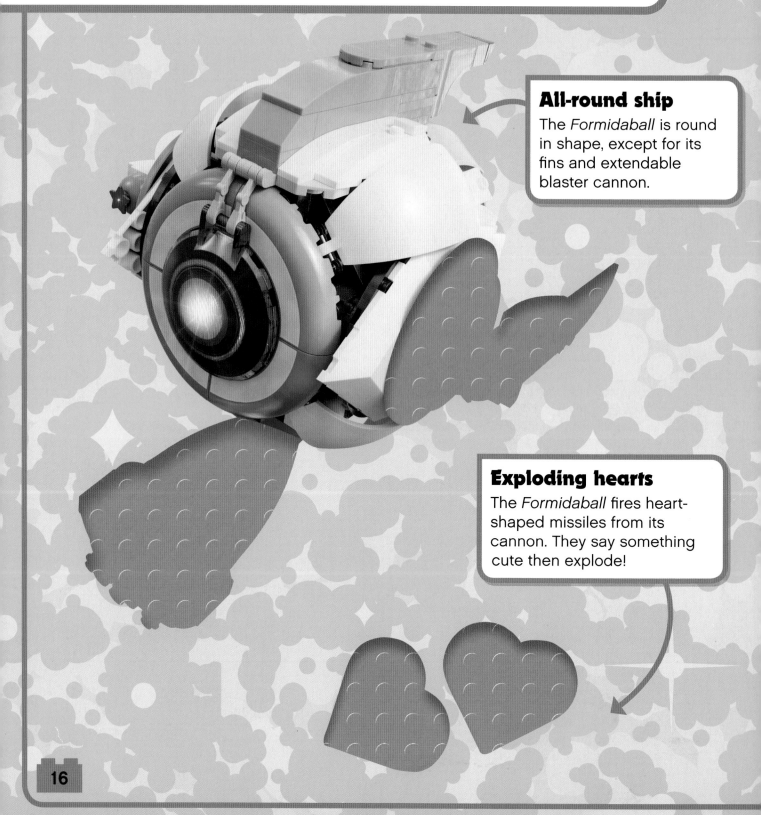

All-round ship

The *Formidaball* is round in shape, except for its fins and extendable blaster cannon.

Exploding hearts

The *Formidaball* fires heart-shaped missiles from its cannon. They say something cute then explode!

Sweet Mayhem is safe inside her ship. The *Formidaball* is covered with ultrastrong armour.

A shooting star?

When Emmet first sees the *Formidaball* in the distance, he thinks it is a shooting star.

In with a bang

The spaceship makes a noisy entrance in Apocalypseburg by shooting out exploding hearts.

MISSION

Sweet Mayhem lands in Apocalypseburg to find the city's fiercest leaders and bring them back to the Systar System. She wastes no time on her mission!

Carried away

It is a tight squeeze on the *Formidaball*. The prisoners do not mind. They enjoy the ride – except for Lucy!

Scooped up

The *Formidaball* scoops up Metalbeard, Benny, Lucy, Batman and Unikitty. They have been kidnapped!

Lucy's escape

Only Lucy feels worried. What does Sweet Mayhem want with them? She looks for a way to escape.

Left behind

Sweet Mayhem does not think Emmet is important enough to kidnap. He is left behind with his houseplant, Planty.

Sweet Mayhem is on a secret mission. She does not tell the friends why she kidnaps them.

To the rescue!

Emmet is determined to rescue his friends. He has the courage. Now he just needs a rocket ship!

REX DANGERVEST

Brave Emmet flies into space to look for his friends. He soon gets into trouble, but a space pilot named Rex helps Emmet out.

Spaceship pro

Rex is a skilful space pilot. He easily flies Emmet's spaceship through a dangerous area known as the Stairgate.

Team of two

After Rex rescues Emmet, the two become friends. Rex agrees to help Emmet find his other friends.

Cool crew

Rex has his own spaceship. When Emmet boards it, he meets its unusual crew. They are all raptor dinosaurs!

Space suit

Rex has a jet suit. He wears it for missions outside his spaceship, such as punching asteroids to pieces.

Skateboard fans

The raptors love skateboarding. Rex's spaceship has a skate park, where they practise kickflips and slides.

Plantimals

During their search, Emmet and Rex meet some Plantimals. Emmet thinks these big-eyed aliens look adorable.

Rex does not think the Plantimals are cute. The creatures use their long vines to trap intruders, like Rex.

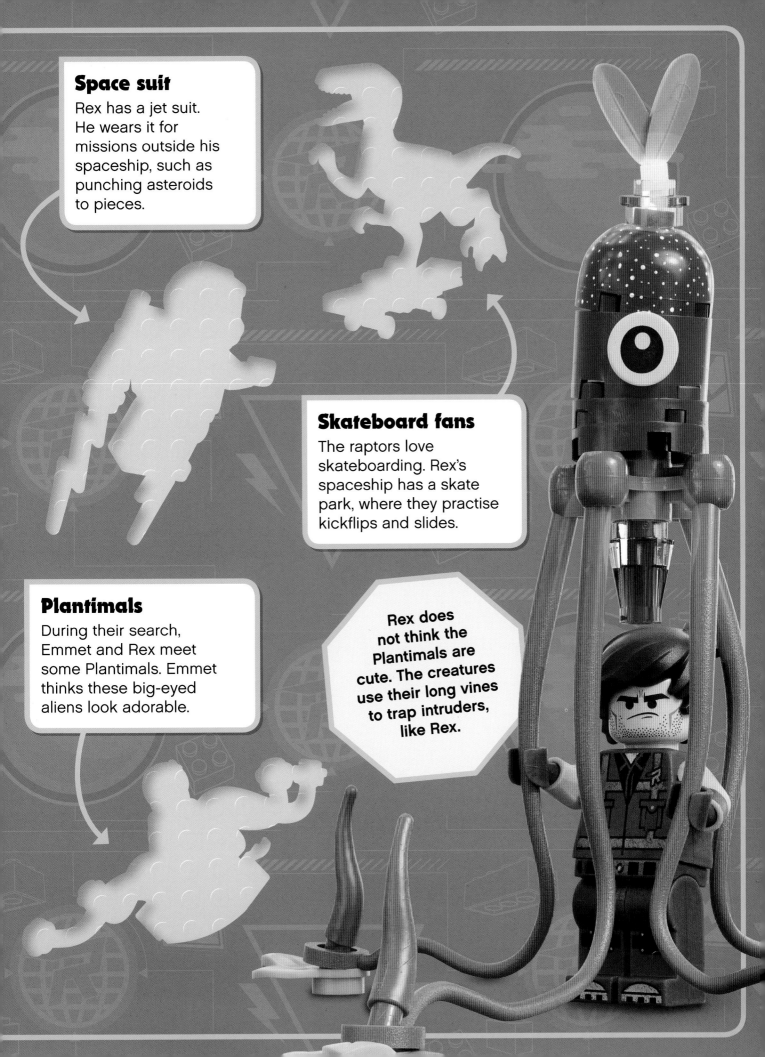

READY, SET, GO!

Getting around Apocalypseburg and the Systar System is easy, fast and fun with these awesome high-tech vehicles.

House rocket

Emmet turns his house into a cool spaceship by adding three giant rocket engines.

The *Rexcelsior*

The *Rexcelsior* is Rex's spaceship. It looks like a huge fist – perhaps because Rex likes to smash things!

Winged raptor

Any raptor can become a high flier. All they need to do is attach a set of high-tech wings.

Flying around

The *Formidaball*'s round shape makes it easy to manoeuvre through space.

Metalbeard's chopper features a very unusual missile launcher. It fires sharks at his enemies!

TRIP INTO SPACE

It's Emmet's first trip into space. He doesn't know what to expect! What will he see out there? Who will he meet?

Use the extra stickers to create your own scene.

SYSTAR SYSTEM

Sweet Mayhem takes the heroes to her home, the Systar System. This cluster of planets is home to things the friends have never seen.

New worlds

The Systar System is made up of many different planets. The friends can't help being impressed as they approach.

Brave explorers

Now that they have landed in the Systar System, the heroes are eager to explore their surroundings.

Jungle planet

This planet is covered in trees and vines. Cute-looking creatures called Plantimals live here.

Spa time

The new arrivals are sent to a special spa to get cleaned up. Unikitty loves how sparkly it is.

Balthazar

An attractive, nonthreatening teen vampire, Balthazar, welcomes the friends to the spa. Namaste!

Zen Bunny loves hanging out in the spa. Daily meditation has turned her into a relaxed rabbit.

QUEEN WATEVRA WA'NABI

Queen Watevra Wa'Nabi reigns over the Systar System. The queen is a shape-shifter, so she can change into any object or animal she chooses.

Shining crown

The queen can arrange her bricks any way she wants. She always wears a gold crown so it is easy to tell that it's her.

Ice Cream Cone

This talking ice-cream cone has a job that's hard to lick! He is the queen's butler.

For a meeting with some alien animal people, the queen takes the form of a horse.

Batman's a fan

Watevra Wa'Nabi uses flattery to get Batman on her side. It works! The Dark Knight decides she's "rad".

First impressions

When Lucy meets the queen, she doesn't trust her. She thinks the queen has a hidden agenda.

Royal gifts

The DUPLO® aliens bring their stolen bricks to the queen. She is building a Space Temple.

Trusted friend

The queen shares all her plans with Sweet Mayhem. She trusts her to keep them secret.

BETTER TOGETHER

There is strength in numbers. Teaming up with friends is a surefire way to make everything awesome! Can friendship unite the galaxy?

Royally awesome

Together, Sweet Mayhem and Queen Watevra Wa'Nabi do their best to make the Systar System an amazing place to live.

Brick together

The DUPLO® aliens work together to take as many bricks as they can from Bricksburg to the queen.

Opposites attract

Rex likes danger. Emmet does not. They are very different, but they become friends anyway.

Raptors united

Running a spaceship is hard work! The close-knit raptor crew keeps the *Rexcelsior* flying high.

Emmet tries to befriend some enemy hearts and stars. They smile back, but can he trust them?

Part of a team

Batman usually likes to work alone. But when his city is attacked, Batman helps his friends defend and rebuild it.

DANCE PARTY

There's nothing better than blasting some tunes and having fun with friends. Who will hit the dance floor?

Use the extra stickers to create your own scene.